HUNGARY
In the Heart of Europe

HUNG

Péter Korniss

Officina Nova

ARY In the Heart of Europe

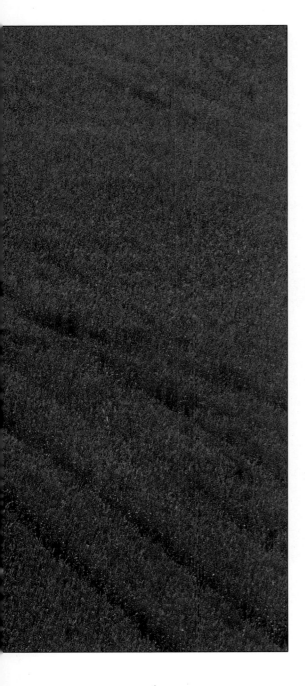

Preface by Árpád Göncz • Introduction by István Nemeskürty

Can a camera lens be objective?

It must be, as it captures only what it sees.

Can a camera lens be partial and subjective?

It must be, as it captures what its owner aims it at.

And the photographer is an artist: he has an established
view of the world. An internal view that he wants
to confirm, even unconsciously, by selecting the subject
of a picture.

Thus the lens is a tool for the artistic rendering
of the world.

A final question: does the lens have sentiments as well?
Such as affection?

Of course it has! Open this book anywhere at random,
and affection radiates from it. The focused affection
of a human life, an artist's life.

Affection for people. For the land that the people
in the pictures call home. For our shared homeland,
Hungary, and for us who, along with the artist, populate
this country. The living subjects of these pictures. Youths
kissing passionately or the elderly living through
– struggling through – two generations. They cannot be
torn from this land, which they learned to see, and which
Péter Korniss learned to make others see.

Göncz Árpád

A backwater of the Danube River near Dunaföldvár

Spring in Tokaj / Winter in the Bükk

Lipizzaner stud in Szilvásvárad

A farmstead in the plains

The nine-arch bridge of Hortobágy

The memorial place of the Muhi battle

CASTLES

were, at the same time, the cradles of culture: thanks to Tamás Nádasdy, a printing shop was established in 1537 in Sárvár, where János Sylvester, later a university professor in Vienna, published a translation of the New Testament with the nobleman's financial support, and Sárospatak provided a home for the famous Reformed (Calvinist) college, still in operation.

The royal palaces differed from the private castles of the aristocrats both in their external appearance and function.

SÜMEG CASTLE

The first castles in the traditional sense, aside from royal seats and county centers, were built in the second half of the 13th century, following the Mongol invasion. These castles served not to guard the border but to enhance the protection and reputation of the owner. From the castle built onto the hill, distant areas could be seen and the work in the fields and merchants' trading could be supervised. The castle at Sümeg, west of Lake Balaton, aptly illustrates this. At the foot of the castle hill, the almost geometrically arranged settlement is visible where when the castle was still in use, people serving the big landowning aristocrats used to live: peasants, gardeners, craftsmen and merchants. The village and the its residents were essentially the property of the castle's master. The Csesznek castle was of similar nature among the forests of the Bakony hill, not far from Veszprém.

These castles in Transdanubia – like the Nagyvázsony castle of Pál Kinizsi, the commander – were built of stone. However, for the castles of the Great Plains, where stone was in short supply, brick was used for construction. Such is the Kisvárda castle in eastern Hungary, or rather its ruins, utilized today as a venue for theatrical performances. Kisvárda used to guard the border between the Transylvanian Principality and Habsburg-held northern Hungary; it frequently changed hands after fierce battles.

The castles of the Renaissance era provided more comfort for its dwellers, as is demonstrated by the Perényi palace in Sárospatak, beautified in the 16th century, or the Nádasdy palace of Sárvár in Transdanubia. The Perényi and Nádasdy families gave their homeland powerful statesmen in the 16th and 17th centuries. Both Sárospatak and Sárvár

SÁROSPATAK

A significant military force was also stationed in them. But these did not function as border fortresses either.

The Diósgyőr castle near Miskolc was a permanent residence of queens, and sometimes the kings resided here,

AND PALACES

for months, on their tours around the country.

The castle of Visegrád on the Danube Bend, in a position providing easy con-

trol over distant areas, was turned into the temporary capital by the Anjou kings of French origin, ruling in the 14th century. King Charles I, King Louis I and his daughter Queen Mary I governed the country from here; Visegrád was often the site of international summit meetings in the Middle Ages. Later, King Matthias Corvinus, who made Buda the country's capital again, built a holiday palace here. Tata, a settlement abundant in waters, was also a royal hunting castle where King Matthias liked to rest after a tiring day of hunting. The adornments of Renaissance taste on the Gothic window frames can be seen in the photo.

The fortress-like character of the oldest monasteries is an unusual feature. These monasteries were built and equipped to resist attacks. This protection was important not so much against foreign enemies but rather to protect the valuables safeguarded in the monastery.

The oldest monastery still operating in Hungary is the castle of Pannonhalma, inhabited by Benedictine monks. Under Saint Stephen's rule, the Benedictine order of monks, founded by Saint Benedict of Italy, cultivated sci-

FERTŐD

ences and also served the king in public administration. The arch-abbot of the monastery acts as a high priest, independent of the country's bishops and archbishops. The monastery of Pannonhalma was founded by King Saint Stephen around the year 1000 to honor Saint Martin – a guard officer in his youth and later the bishop of Tours, France – born in the Roman era in Savaria (today Szombat-

hely in Transdanubia or Pannonia). The king never launched a war without asking for the protection of Saint Martin. The Benedictine monastery, named after Saint Martin, gained the poetic name Pannonhalma only in the 19th century; before that it was called Saint Martin's Hill.

In the course of the 18th century, the nobility left their castles and moved to more comfortable palaces. Such is the palace of the great statesman and writer Count István Széchenyi in Nagycenk; the palace of the Esterházy princes in Fertőd (called Esterháza until 1949) and the palace of the Festetics princes in Keszthely. Each of the palaces is surrounded by neatly planned parks, and magnificent music halls provide concert opportunities. The Eszterházy princes sponsored the composer Haydn. The Festetics family generously supported Hungarian literature.

The ruins of Csesznek Castle

The Visegrád Castle
with the Danube

The Nagyvázsony Castle

43

The adorned gate and richly
furnished rooms
of the palace of the Festetics
princes in Keszthely

Concert in the Festetics Palace

The ancient crypt
and Gothic cloister
of the Pannonhalma Abbey

The library of the abbey
with the sculpture of Saint Stephen

The main gate
of the Fertőd Palace

THE VILLAGE

HORTOBÁGY

FOLK HOUSE IN BARANYA

The Hungarian village is an agricultural community with family-owned single-story houses, huge gardens and hay fields in the plains; with enclosed gardens in the hilly areas and tiny flower gardens in front of the house. Every village had craftsmen but not of all trades. However, each of the villages kept smiths and boot-makers. The cooper, the barrel maker, was indispensable to vineyard areas. The church was usually built on a hill in the center of the village. As a separate settlement, a row of cellars stretched on the outskirts of the villages in fruit and vineyard areas, where the family moved to during vintage time or in the summer heat. A northern Hungarian village, Hollókő, hidden among hills and so preserved its ancient character untouched. It has been declared a protected area, a living museum. Similarly, a few dozen settlements of the Őrség in southwestern Hungary were preserved in their ancient state under the strict guardianship of forest-covered hills. As its name indicates, the Őrség was a region of guards: it was inhabited by soldiers' families who settled here in the Middle Ages to guard the borders. Since the area remained independent from counties and landlords, no castles, palaces or landlord's mansions were built here. The families lived independent lives, not compelled even to serve as serfs. The Őrség region spread to the areas that became part of Austria in 1920 (Burgenland), where some Hungarians still live today. The seat of the Austrian Őrség is Felsőőr (Oberwart). The picture of Szalafő presents a typical thatch-roofed dwelling in the Őrség. The thatched roof had long been in nationwide use and as it turned out, proved to be a useful, healthy, insulating yet ventilating type of roof. The house walls built of sun-dried clay bricks also proved effective. The picture taken in Nagytótfalu, Baranya County, presents the most characteristic building style in the country:

the apartments are separated from the court by a covered corridor-type space divided by columns. There is a well in the courtyard, covered by a wooden roof to protect it from bad weather. The houses were generally whitewashed; this was an effective method of preventing disease, since lime is a disinfectant. Yellowish whitewash – mixed with a kind of yellow clay – was rarer; it is visible on the house on Petőfi Street in Drávapalkonya.

The annual country fair, coupled with a bazaar, was a village festivity. Showmen set up their tents and the merry-go-round whirled. The day of the country fair was also the celebration of the village's patron saint. Every church and parish (where the births, christening ceremonies, weddings and deaths were registered) had a patron saint for whom some relic was hidden in the altar. On the patron saint's day, the population of the village (primarily in Catholic settlements; this habit is being abandoned in Calvinist villages) attended a mass, after which they swarmed out to the spacious area along the village border where marketers, honey-cake makers,

furriers, meat roasters, boot-makers and potters lined up.

Generally, the churches are impressive buildings, maintained by the population and the priest with great care. If the church had no bell tower, an adjacent belfry was scaffolded. One example is the bell tower of Nagyszekeres in Szatmár in eastern Hungary. Here in Szatmár, then in Bereg and up in the Bodrogköz near the Tisza River, the conquering Hungarians who arrived from the Verecke pass first settled. These places have preserved the oldest traditions. For example, in the Szatmárcseke cemetery (the estate of the

THE REFORMED CHURCH IN NAGYSZEKERES

great Hungarian poet Ferenc Kölcsey, the author of the Hungarian national anthem), for a thousand years, without interruption, people erected tomb-posts carved in the shape of a boat, in remem-

HOLLÓKŐ

brance of the deceased who sailed to the other world on Charon's boat. The faithful village people erected a statue of the village's patron saint or most frequently, a

statue of the Virgin Mary in the nearby fields along the roads.

In villages ruled by the landlord, the aristocrats – in competition with each other – built luxurious churches, equals of the most fashionable Western European, primarily French, styles of the time. The country is resplendent with such masterpieces, such as the Benedictine church of Ják. The church was consecrated by the Bishop of Győr in 1256. A smaller, movingly beautiful church is the one in Velemér. Its frescoes, impressive even in their shabbiness, tell sacred stories to the illiterate faithful coming in and looking around the church.

After the burden of workdays (mowing, animal tending, sheep watering) the villagers, wearing festive outfits, sometimes ancient folk costumes, celebrate the great holidays (such as Easter or Corpus Christi) by processions leading out into the countryside. One picture depicts the Easter festivities of Orthodox Gypsies in the village of Hodász in the Nyírség region. Birth, death, wedding and burial – festivities following the eternal cycle and rebirth of nature.

Among the Zala Hills

Wine-press houses in Villánykövesd

A typically Hungarian form of settlement:
a village in the Nyírség

Wine cellars in Palkonya

Modern architecture with an eye on the past in Nagykálló

Village street in the Bakony

The community house in Nagykálló

A peasant house in the Őrség

The Ják church

Hollókő, a village
of the World Heritage

Work in the fields

Grazing

"Busó" procession in Mohács

Easter open-air mass in Hodász

The Lord's Day procession
in Rimóc
of those taking their
First Communion

In the fair

In the Rimóc Church

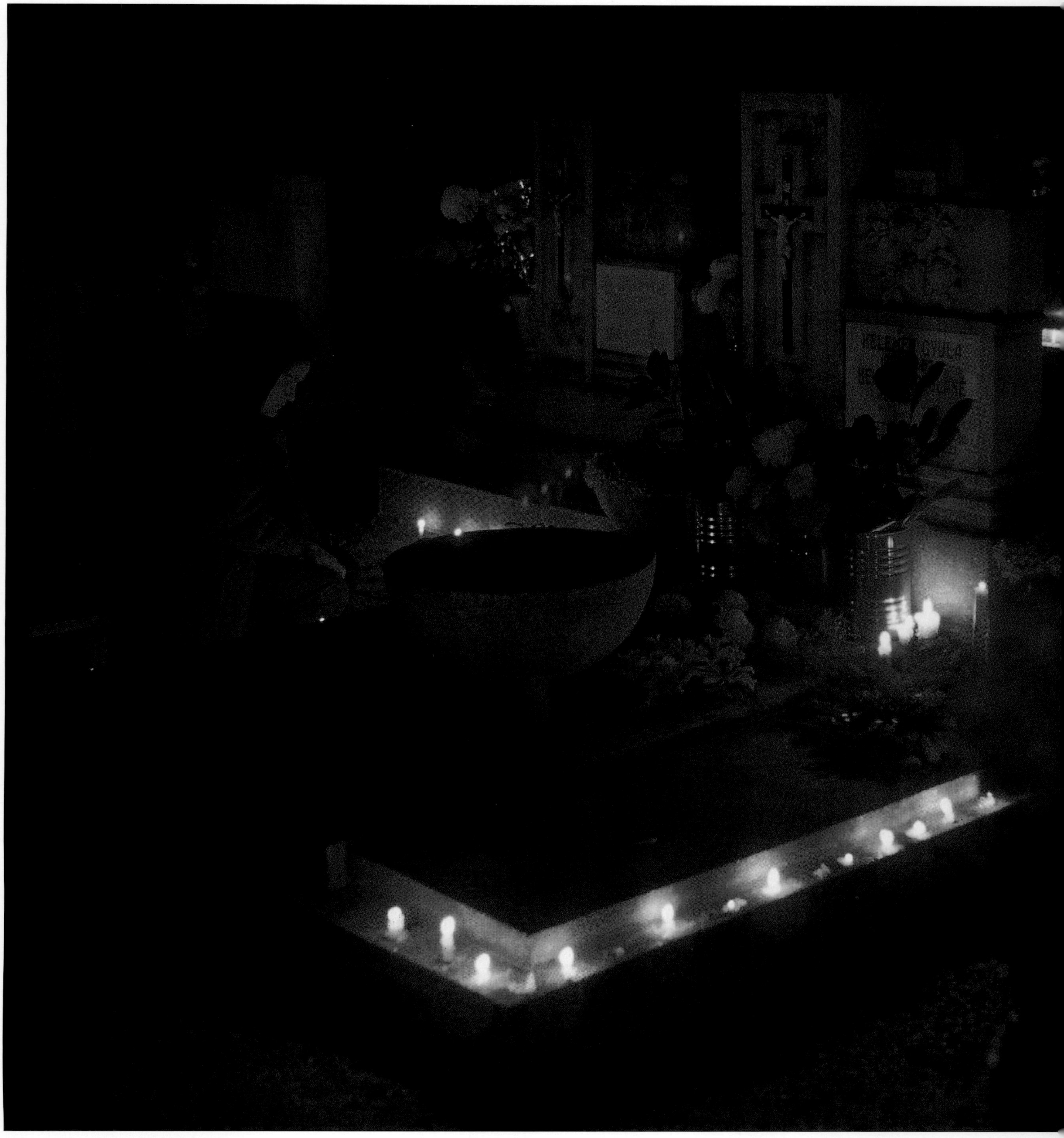
GYULA

The Szatmárcseke Cemetery

DEBRECEN

development of the past 50 years altered the old townscape and the big housing estates changed the town's character. Pécs, Esztergom and Eger however, preserved their ancient appearance. Pécs is unusual in that while the monumental cathedral with four towers is situated in the middle of a beautiful park, a few hundred meters away on the main square, a Turkish mosque has been transformed into a Catholic church, its ancient architectural features preserved. Of the episcopal towns however, Eger cherishes the ornate taste of the enlightened 18th century: the victory of modern sciences has been immortalized in Sigrit's frescoes, painted at the end of the 18th century in the episcopal school and library. Eger Castle, once an episcopal castle-fortress and cathedral, today attracts thousands of visitors with the relics of the fortress system. This castle, far from any

The towns of Hungary – with the exception of episcopal, principal and county seats – developed in the 13th century. The bourgeoisie became rich and organized into a political force in the 14th century. From then on, kings accepted them as their allies against the nobles and they received free royal town titles. Nobles were not even allowed to move into a free royal town without permission.

In design, administration and appearance, the towns of Transdanubia and northern Hungary rival Western European towns. Some Transdanubian towns are of Roman origin, such as Óbuda (Aquincum), Pécs (Sopianae) and Szombathely (Savaria). One photo in this album depicts the stone road of Szombathely built by the Romans about 1600 years ago.

The centers and main attractions of the towns are their main squares. Churches are also important, but these were centrally

SÁROSPATAK

placed only in episcopal towns (Esztergom, Pécs and Eger). The episcopal church and castle of Veszprém, built on a hill, is also centrally positioned but the

border, was besieged in 1552 by the Turkish sultan's huge army, but the few thousand defenders resisted successfully. In memory of this victory, Eger has become

THE TOWN

_____ SZOMBATHELY _____

ic church and fin-de-siècle architecture stand near the sculpture of Lajos Kossuth, the hero of the War of Independence.

It is intriguing how self-consciously the small towns follow the latest architectural trends. Paks and Siófok asked Imre Makovecz to build their churches; these buildings are masterpieces of organic architectural style. A housing complex in Sárospatak, decorative in spite of its affectation, is characteristically up-to-date.

The towns of the plains developed dif-

building in a spread-out village pattern. This is how these cities grew big. Otherwise, Kecskemét, for example, became prosperous through major exports of cattle, and huge pastures were required for animal husbandry (Bugac). Debrecen developed similarly, the only difference being that the town never came under direct Turkish rule. Thus its cultural institutions (a college, a printing house) were also more developed. Kecskemét outdoes itself with the colorful, turn-of-the-centu-

the symbol of successful military and national resistance.

Of the burgher's towns of Transdanubia, Pécs, Kőszeg and Sopron managed to preserve their old townscape the most, although Sopron was hit by devastating air strikes in the early summer of 1945, as was Szombathely, where only traces of the old town are visible. Tiny Kőszeg however, with its town hall adorned with a coat-of-arms and a Madonna, and its unexpectedly turning and winding streets – to cause the enemy to lose his way in them – gives the impression of a movie set.

For decades Miskolc, in northern Hungary, was the second largest town in the country. Its architecture is interesting in that its housing estates, built one after the other, and its hasty construction projects at the beginning of the century remind one of American towns. However, a Goth-

_____ MISKOLC _____

ferently from cities in western Hungary. Debrecen, Szeged and Kecskemét are major peasant towns. Kecskemét and Szeged were ruled by the Turkish sultan for one-and-a-half centuries. The dwellers of the tiny villages fled to the towns for safety and swelled them by following their traditional architectural style,

ry facades in the Hungarian Secessionist style, while Szeged gained its present form through a votive church, a square around it and the university building complex built after a catastrophic flood in the past century. Open-air theater performances are held on the square in front of the cathedral every summer.

Medieval houses in Sopron

A street in Sopron

The medieval main square in Sopron

A view of Győr

In downtown Székesfehérvár

Eger Castle: the legendary site
of the fight against the Turks

The fresco in the Lyceum's library

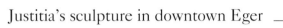

Justitia's sculpture in downtown Eger

Mass in the Esztergom Basilica

103

Szentendre moments

The
Evangelical
Church
in Siófok:
a master-
piece
of organic
architecture

The Pécs Cathedral with the castle wall

Street section with a fountain in Pécs

The Cifra Palace in Kecskemét   A church section in Paks

Storno House
in Sopron

The chapel
of Esztergom
Castle

The facade
of the Szeged
Cathedral

A Baroque street
section in Eger

_____ Seagulls above the lake

Play

A hotel on the Aranypart
(Golden Shore)

The Tihany peninsula
with the inner lake

The lake at Örvényes

_____ The ice-covered Füred bay

Sailboats taking a rest
at Balatonalmádi

The Parliament building

The towers of the Saint Anne Church, the Danube River
and the Margaret Bridge in the background

The Hotel Hilton, the Fisherman's Bastion
and the church on Szilágyi Dezső Square

Baroque castle gate,
with statue of Eugene of Savoy
(on horseback) in the background

The palace in Buda Castle, housing the National Gallery

Matthias Church   The medieval castle chapel

A courtyard in Dísz Square

149

Snow-covered courtyard
in Fortuna Street

Winter on Margaret Island

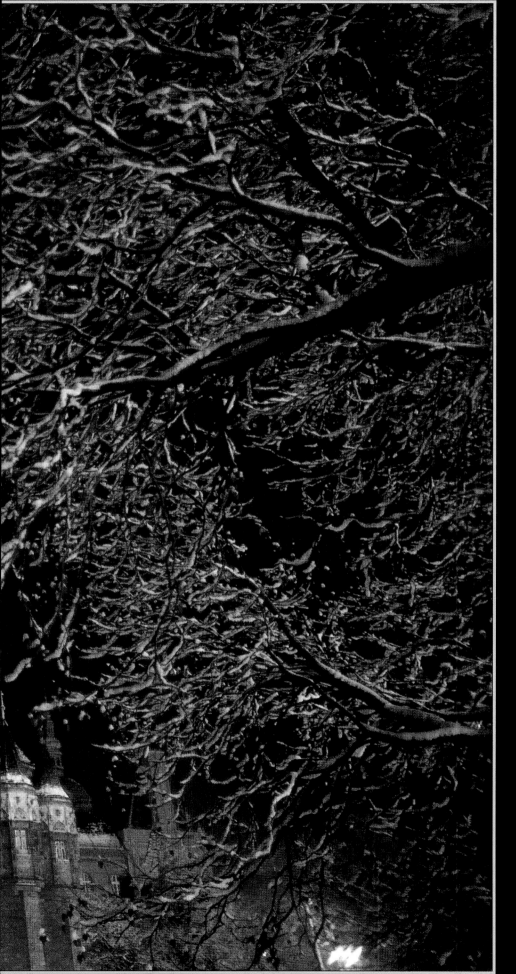

Vajdahunyad Castle in Városliget

The well of the Nereids
on Ferenciek Square

An ornament adorning
a Neo-Renaissance apartment
house on Andrássy Avenue

The sculptures of the Basilica

The Dohány Street Synagogue

A masterpiece of Hungarian Secessionism:
the Museum of Applied Arts

The sculptures of the Vigadó

A staircase in a downtown house

Caryatids on Andrássy Avenue

A balcony in the Józsefváros District

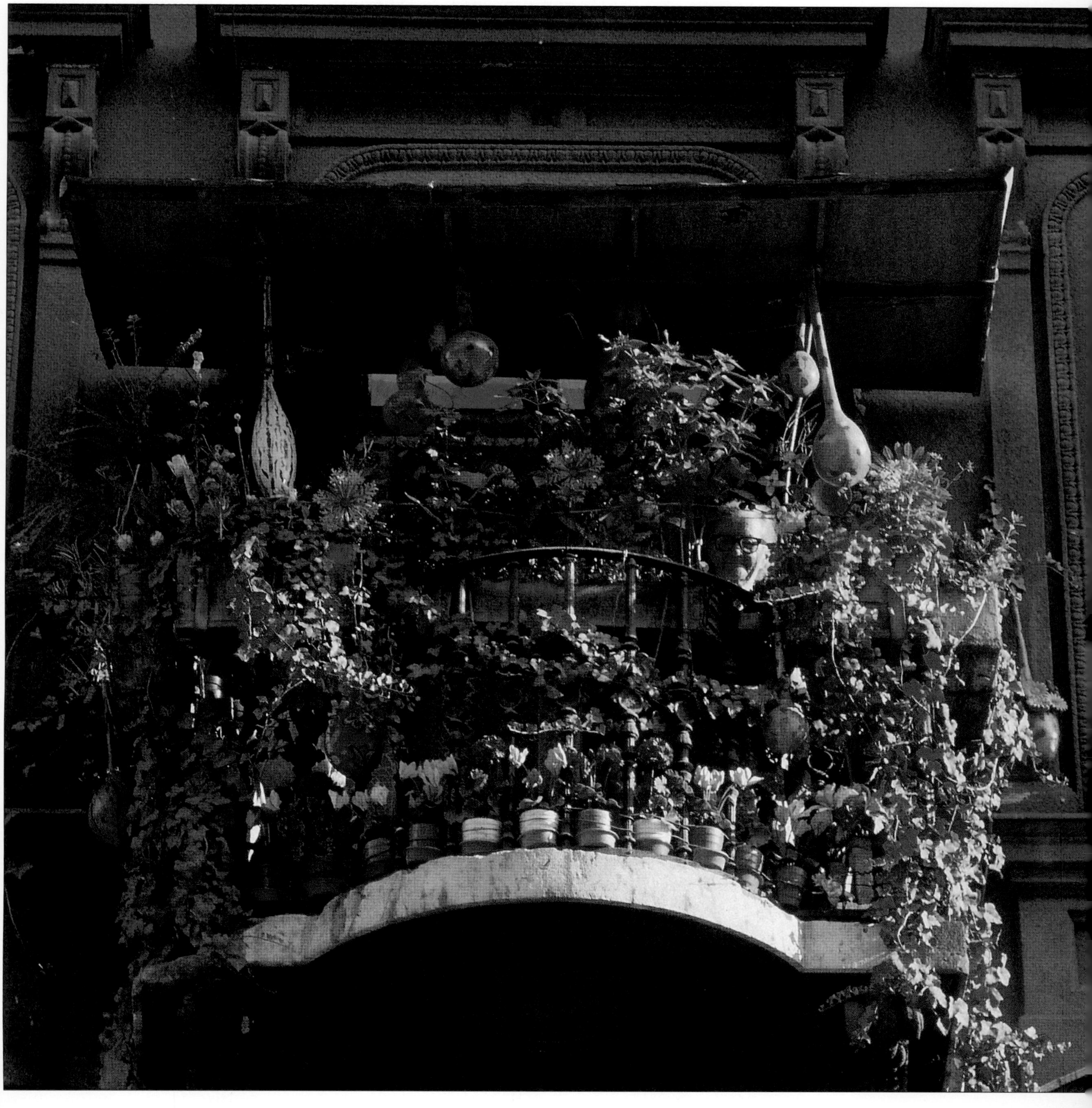

Graduation celebration

The New York Café

A turn-of-the-century carousel
in the Városliget

The Saint Stephen Boulevard in late afternoon

Heroes' Square

Designer: Julianna Rácz / 9s műhely

Translated by Gabriella Schön

Language editor: Chris Springer

Initiated by the Kreatív Média Workshop

Producer: József Böjte

Magyar Könyvklub, Budapest, 2000

Publisher: Gábor Révai

Typesetting by 9s műhely

Printing by Kossuth Printing House

ISBN 963 547 184 X